MW01046825

Discipling the Generation: A Directed Study

Chris A. Legebow

Copyright © 2017 Chris A. Legebow

All rights reserved.

ISBN-13: 978-1-988914-09-1

DEDICATION

I thank God for the teachers and pastors who imparted spiritual truths, investing in my spiritual life. It is my prayer that you will also pass these truths on to others.

CONTENTS

Acknowledgments i

1 Introduction 6

2 First Contact 19

3 Holy Spirit Led Learning 22

4 Truths of Healing 26

5 Communion 30

6 Spiritual Desire 35

7 Baptism of the Holy Spirit 38

8 Covenants of God 45

9 Foot washing 49

10 God's Word 53

11 Anointing with Oil 57

12 Conclusion 60

13 Journal Topics 65

ACKNOWLEDGMENTS

All Scripture taken from Biblegateway.com
Modern English version (MEV)

1 INTRODUCTION

In the early 1990's I watched Lester Summerall, a mighty man of God who preached all over the earth, lay hands imparting a blessing onto Rod Parsely and his wife Joni. He literally had a sword and passed it to him as a symbolic gesture. It didn't stop there. He began to pray in English and in tongues that God would pour out His Spirit on Rod Parsely and that all the anointing that was on his life would be imparted into Rod Parsley. He is a gifted Evangelist and leader of a Church. What occurred was supernatural both Rod Parsley and Joni were filled with the Spirit ot overflowing and both were slain in the Spirit. Lester Summerall continued prophesying over them as they lay there on the ground. I was praying with them. I realized I was witnessing the passing of a legacy. I knew that Spiritually a new anointing was coming on Rod Parsley and his ministry.

I began to consider the transferring of the anointing of Elijah and Elisha. It impressed me so strongly of the importance of passing on the truths of God to those who will run after us. At my church, one of the ministers preached on that topic and I knelt at my seat and made an altar and prayed for the anointing of the double portion blessing. I prayed for it with all my being. I wanted more of God than I could even imagine. God and I knew what it was about. No one else knew how I had prayed that day. It was as important an altar in my life as any of the major decisions I've made since salvation. It was a turning point. I knew that the anointing of the Holy Spirit has a tangible presence as real as any physical object. I wanted the double portion as Elisha did.

2 Kings 2: 7 Fifty men of the sons of the prophets went and stood at a distance, and the two of them stood by the Jordan. 8 Then Elijah took his robe and rolled it up and struck the water, and it was divided from one side to the other. Then the two of them crossed on dry ground.

9 And as they were crossing, Elijah said to Elisha, "Ask for something, and I will do it for you before I am taken away from you."

And Elisha said, "Let a double portion of your spirit be upon me."

10 He said, "You have asked for a difficult thing, but if you see me when I am taken from you, it will happen to you. If not, it will not."

11 As they continued walking and talking, a chariot of fire and horses of fire separated the two of them, and Elijah went up by a whirlwind into heaven.

12 Elisha was watching and crying, "My father, my father, the chariot of Israel and its horsemen!" And he did not see him again. Then he grabbed his own clothes and tore them in two pieces.

13 He picked up the robe of Elijah that fell from him, and he returned and stood on the bank of the Jordan. 14 And he took the robe of Elijah that fell from him, and struck the water, and said, "Where is the Lord, God of Elijah?" When he had struck the water, it parted from one side to the other, and Elisha crossed over.

The impartation of the anointing

The passing on of the anointing became a fascination of mine. I got books on the topic. I listened to any preaching on the topic. I have only heard excellent preaching on the topic several occasions. I myself have studied it in detail and depth. I believe it is important because what we leave as a legacy in the earth can be significant if we can disciple people, pray and impart blessings to them.

It was several years later that Benny Hinn was preaching in Lansing Michigan. I drove some friends to the Crusade. I made a special point of going, not only because it was good but because I had a close friend with cancer. I went to pray and stand in prayer receiving for her. The praise and worship was beautiful. Anyone who has ever been in a Benny Hinn meeting knows the praise and worship and the anointing of faith that is in the atmosphere. There were more than 20, 000 people there. We had seats way up in one of the top baloneys. I was glad to be there at all because I had to work and made it anyway. There were waves of the moving of the Holy Spirit throughout the congregation. All the people there with me, Jeff, Cherene, Sue were slain in the Spirit – in the top Balcony! I felt the strong presence of God but was not slain in the spirit. There were people all around the packed auditorium getting slain in the Spirit during the praise and the worship. Pastor Benny spoke on the double portion anointing and I could barely contain myself. It was as though I had come not only for my friend, but God was blessing me in a special way also. It was a perk.

During the altar call, probably more than 15, 000 people tried to go forward. All the aisles were blocked. I got several rows from the platform. I wanted the blessings he was praying over the congregation and I wanted God to know I was serious. I was surrounded by people I didn't know. It didn't matter. I wanted all of what God would give me. As I yielded to the Holy Spirit, I knew God's presence was on me strong. I knew God heard my silent prayers. I yielded my life. All the people around me were falling to the ground. I stood there like a beacon. I kind of wondered about it. I knew I had given all myself to God and I believed by faith that God heard me and would give it to me. I stood in the Holy Presence of God soaking in the presence of God. I returned to my seat.

The Crusade was between 3-5 hours long. Most of it was worship, prayer and testimonies of healing. As my friends and I started towards the car, they were talking about how God had touched them. Cherene felt God touch her knee. Sue (who didn't believe in being slain in the Spirit) was slain in the spirit. Even Jeff was slain in the Spirit. I had a moment of "God why did you miss me?" enter my thoughts and God immediately replied – "You didn't pray to be slain in the Spirit. You prayed for the double portion anointing." I realized and immediately repented for coveting their special experience. All the way home they talked about it. I was now happy for them because God had corrected me and I had a proper attitude.

I prayed for my friend Sheri and believe God knew it and accepted it as I was standing in proxy for her. Thousands of people were praying for her literally. She was completely healed of cancer. I believe I received my heart's prayer those altar calls. I believe God gave me my heart's desire. I wanted more God than I could imagine. God has given me so many opportunities to receive much excellent teaching and preaching. First of all, my Michigan Churches had important Prophets, Apostles, Evangelists, Teacher's and Pastors come and speak in person. I had privilege to receive directly from those people. I knew it was a special blessing. I knew it was possibly once in a life kind of experience. I pressed into God with all my being. Any preachers I could talk to, I talked to; I received words of encouragement. Sometimes I got prayed for in person. Sometimes I simply stood and listened. Part of receiving the double portion anointing means you give yourself to learn from others who have more experience. Many of the ministers had lived through the Latter Rain Revival of the 1940's- 50's. I treasured their preaching, taking notes, often buying the tapes.

It was normal for me to listen to the preaching tapes over and over throughout the week so the Word of God got into the insides of me. I knew I must have more of God. My spiritual mentors – really like Spiritual parents had invested much of what they knew into me. They always talked about Minister's Candidate school and how it changed their lives. It was no longer offered at our church though because the minister wasn't there anymore. As soon as my friend Roseanne told me the Pastor at her church was teaching Minister's Candidate school my ears perked up. I said though that I didn't just want any old minister's candidate school. I wanted the same one that had been at our church. She said that her Pastor received his training at the minister's candidate that was at our Church. I immediately started asking about it. It became a strong passion to me. I yearned to know more of God. The course I desired was being offered.

Through Minister's Candidate school, we received preaching and teaching, wrote exams, did volunteer ministry, attended services, received training. I did not want to miss one day. It started as a Saturday and Wednesday thing. To complete my certificate, I had to also take classes offered on other days. Jeff took some classes. Cherene took some classes. None of us were together. We all chose different paths. I believe the practical hands on aspect of the education helped me to become a more mature Christian as well as give me knowledge. The laying on of hands ceremony at the end was not just ceremony. It was an impartation confirming the truths that had been taught to us but also prophesying about our future. I received blessing from ministers who had been in revival and were missionaries as well as prophets. I received ministry from my Pastor/teacher also. In my final year in 1994, I was teaching a small group in the minister's Candidate class. It was my joy. I found my place. I never thought I would leave. I wanted to stay there praying for people and teaching them the things that had been taught to me.

Investing in others means a commitment of your life as well as your resources. It means discipleship at a deeper level. I have received, and I knew I must give. I feel so strongly that I must impart to others, sometimes it is overwhelming. I know that God did not give me the truths I have learned to hoard them. What you receive freely you must also give.

Matthew 10: 7 As you go, preach, saying, 'The kingdom of heaven is at hand.' 8 Heal the sick, cleanse the lepers, raise the dead, and cast out demons. Freely you have received, freely give.

In the early 2000's until 2005, I had opportunity to train college and career as well as youth 12 – 13-year-old children. I not only taught the classes but invested in their lives. Often, I would invite people to my home or go to their homes sharing and teaching and imparting Christ. I believe it is God's will for me to be imparting to teens, 20 somethings, 30 somethings and anyone who wants to know more of God. This book is a manual that you can use to help you to disciple the generation we live in. It is my hope and prayer that you adopt a youth person from your Church and give yourself to train that person in the things of God. It can happen. Usually the person will come to you or God will place you together. Mentoring the generation is the more popular term but it is really discipling the generation. You are teaching the things God has taught you because you know it will be passed on to people who will pass it on to others. It is God's way of training up others.

Purpose of my book

This book is not a replacement for the foundations of the Christian faith. It is not for new believers. It is for Christians who would mentor the generation of youth that are Christians but that do not have experience with the things of God. There are people who are in full gospel churches going to full gospel services with no gifts of the Holy Spirit present in the Church! I don't say this to criticize but to point out the necessity of sharing the things we have learned lest the Church become a yacht club or a social place only. We who know the Holy Spirit must impart to those who do not. It is not the job of only the Pastors or the elders. Mature Christians can do it.

The book will guide you through things that are important to the full gospel Spirit Baptized Charismatic, Pentecost life. It's not natural. It's supernatural. I am sure that as you invest in a person, you yourself will be strengthened and established and refreshed. There is a special anointing that comes upon a person to impart to others. I pray that anointing be on you so that as you meet with and pour into a youth, you will impart to the spirit of the person as well as teach things.

The purpose of my book is so that it can be used as a training manual to instruct someone in the necessary aspects of our Christian Charismatic Pentecostal faith. It can be for personal self-improvement but the ultimate goal is that it be used to disciple others. It is meant for a one on one or small group mentoring relationship.

Sowing and Reaping

What you sow into the lives of people will multiply in your own life. As we give, God multiplies the supply and the seed sown. You may know this to be true of finances because it is usually used as a text for that topic. It is also a true principle of the spirit that applies to all types of giving, Directly sowing into someone's life truths of the kingdom of God will multiply the seed sown. As the person receives the truth and draws it from you, not only is that person blessed by your giving, but the anointing on you to minister is multiplied. God will give you words of wisdom in your mouth and scriptures that will roll from your spirit that you won't even understand or that may teach you. Your spirit is quickened by the anointing. Your spirit is quickened by spiritually giving. When someone receives from your spiritual gifts within you it draws more of the presence of God to you. That person's faith places a demand for spiritual refreshment.

As you invest in someone's life, it always produces fruit in the person and in yourself. 30, 60, 100-FOLD.

Matthew 13: 8 But other seeds fell into good ground and produced grain: a hundred, sixty, or thirty times as much. 9 Whoever has ears to hear, let him hear."

Matthew 13: 23 But he who received seed on the good ground is he who hears the word and understands it, who indeed bears fruit. Some produce a hundred, sixty, or thirty times what was sown."

The receiver of the truths may receive according to his or her faith. The person may also receive by the gift of faith. I am trying to explain that the human spirit is not like a physical container. The spirit is fluid and it is possible to pull more from a person than the person knows in the natural. The Holy Spirit can give the teacher a word of wisdom or word of knowledge and a whole new dimension of faith is excited because of it. Rather than linear growth, it can be multidimensional and exponential.

Godly life

Many people can become Christians and possibly never grow beyond the initial salvation experience. It is possible to stop learning about spiritual things because it isn't taught or practiced in the congregation. It is possible

to not know what you are missing because you didn't realize how awesome our God is.

A godly man's life is characterized by fruits of righteousness. These are characteristics of Christ imparted into a person through constant abiding in God's presence. You can impart spiritual gifts and anointing for ministry. You cannot impart spiritual fruit. Understanding the need for spiritual fruit is like learning to like spinach or Brussel sprouts. They are necessary to help you to develop a healthy life. A person's life is like a tree of righteousness. The image is used throughout the Bible.

Tree of Righteousness,

Psalm 1: 2 but his delight is in the law of the Lord,
   and in His law he meditates day and night.
3 He will be like a tree planted by the rivers of water,
   that brings forth its fruit in its season;
its leaf will not wither,
   and whatever he does will prosper.

A tree of righteousness planted by living waters is like a man who lives his life living in the Holy Spirit and being lead by the Spirit of God. It always has a supply of water to give it life. It always bears fruit. Its leaves will always be healthy. A person planted in God's foundations who gives himself to prayer, Spiritual growth and following the leading of the Spirit is always going to flourish. The person will always be successful because God is the source he draws from.

Tree of Righteousness

Salvation

In Isaiah the analogy to a tree of righteousness is used once more. The truth of why the anointing is on your life is explained in much detail. The anointing is on your life to preach the good news of salvation. The presence of God is on you, so you can share Christ with others. The anointing is on you to bring salvation, healing to those who are broken-hearted.

Healing of the heart

The anointing of God on a person can heal a broken heart. I know it is radical. Hopefully you yourself have experienced the peace of God that passes all human understanding at the death of a loved one or after a divorce or other such tragedy of life. God's anointing, the flowing of the Spirit of God can heal that person so that not even a scar remains. Such radical teaching doesn't exist outside of the church because there is no human cure for a broken heart. There is no known way to bring inner healing to people. By the anointing of God, it not only can occur, it does occur. If someone who is saved in church is never taught that God binds up and heals the broken hearted, the person may remain wounded and live less of a life than he could live if someone had only preached the truth to him.

Deliverance

The anointing can deliver those who are in bondage to sin or addictions. I mean an addict can be set free. Someone who was in bondage to sin can be set free, so he will not want it any more nor need it. It is radical teaching. It is what God's word promises us. We should be teaching our youth they do not have to be addicted to anything.

Joy

There is a level of joy and celebration of a person living in the spirit that words cannot explain. There is a high in serving God and living in personal relationship with God higher than any alcohol or drug or chemical. The high that comes from the Most High God can be imitated by those things but it can never be reproduced. Only God is a living being who lives on the inside of you and can bring quickening or a wellspring of life. It isn't simply a human chemical thing. It is the spirit of God. The Holy Spirit filling your spirit causes you to be transformed from glory to glory. Living with God and letting the Holy Spirit direct you, aligning your life with God's Word is the sure way of living beyond what you could have imagined for yourself. Instead of your own human experience determining your potential, you align with Almighty God's promises that include supernatural life for you, blessing, prosperity, peace, and joy.

Isaiah 61:1 The Spirit of the Lord God is upon me
     because the Lord has anointed me
     to preach good news to the poor;
He has sent me to heal the broken-hearted,
     to proclaim liberty to the captives,
     and the opening of the prison to those who are bound;
2 to proclaim the acceptable year of the Lord
     and the day of vengeance of our God;
to comfort all who mourn,
3   to preserve those who mourn in Zion,
to give to them beauty
     for ashes,
the oil of joy
     for mourning,
the garment of praise
     for the spirit of heaviness,
that they might be called trees of righteousness,
     the planting of the Lord,
     that He might be glorified.

Once more the tree analogy is used in the book of John with Jesus' own words saying that if you abide in Him and His words abide in you, you will certainly bear spiritual fruit that remains.

John 15: 4 Remain in Me, as I also remain in you. As the branch cannot bear fruit by itself, unless it remains in the vine, neither can you, unless you remain in Me.

5 "I am the vine, you are the branches. He who remains in Me, and I in him, bears much fruit. For without Me you can do nothing. 6 If a man does not remain in Me, he is thrown out as a branch and withers

7If you remain in Me, and My words remain in you, you will ask whatever you desire, and it shall be done for you. 8 My Father is glorified by this, that you bear much fruit; so you will be My disciples.

Finally, in the book of Revelation the tree analogy is used to describe the trees in heaven that are planted on both sides of the river of the Holy Spirit. It describes not only a natural tree that usually bears fruit once but an ever-bearing tree that produces fruit each month. A tree that bears fruit every month is like a miracle tree. The tree not only produces leaves and flowers, but bears fruit every month! That's the type of tree of righteousness I want to be. Planted in God, is the start. The Holy Spirit is our source and nourishment. It is possible to be bearing fruit each month rather than once a season. There is an exponential surreal type of bearing going on. If there is a need for the fruit, the fruit produces. If there is a need for healing, the leaves of the tree produce healing. It is most certainly symbolic, but it is also spiritual. Pray that God may use you to be an ever-bearing tree as you invest into the life of someone. Pray that whatever is necessary will manifest and God will quicken you.

Revelation 22: 1 Then he showed me a pure river of the water of life, clear as crystal, flowing from the throne of God and of the Lamb 2 in the middle of its street. On each side of the river was the tree of life, which bore twelve kinds of fruit, yielding its fruit each month. The leaves of the tree were for the healing of the nations. Without faith, these are just words. First you must believe. You must stir up your faith to impart it. You must speak it with conviction. God rewards those who diligently seek Him.

Hebrews 11: 6 And without faith it is impossible to please God, for he who comes to God must believe that He exists and that He is a rewarder of those who diligently seek Him.

You may invest in a family member. Certainly, it is excellent and can be used for it. It is also my hope that you will invest in someone who you adopt spiritually, even if it only for a season. It can be someone you know. It can be a friend's son or daughter. It can be someone you meet at Church but sense a connection or a willingness to learn from God. I recommend highly it be men with boys and women with girls, but you can do it differently if you and your spouse are present. I would hope to use this book in a church setting. It can be offered as a class option, but it will be you and the candidate or you and your spouse and the candidate. It is meant to be a 6 month – 9 month commitment of once a month. It can be more frequent, once a week for several months. The point is that there a continual getting together for spiritual growth to occur. There should be the development of trust so that you can share spiritual truths with them. As you and your spouse and the candidate meet together, a relationship will develop of teacher and student. God will give you wisdom beyond your own self to speak explaining the scriptures and in knowing how to reach the candidate.

Such a sacred trust should be guarded and honoured.

You will reap what you sow. The first thing is to sow something of spiritual life into the person. You don't just start doing it like putting on a CD or DVD. Once a relationship begins, God will lead you to invest in the youth's life. Invest first in gaining trust. Next find out what the person needs. You can only do it through the Holy Spirit directly you. Included are sample lessons that you can use in your meetings, but you may change them as you desire to more effectively witness to the person.

Galatians 6: 7 Be not deceived. God is not mocked. For whatever a man sows, that will he also reap. 8 For the one who sows to his own flesh will from the flesh reap corruption, but the one who sows to the Spirit will from the Spirit reap eternal life.

Jesus gave us authority

Jesus gave us all authority to impart and disciple the nations. That includes you and me. If for some reason you should doubt yourself believing that you have nothing to impart but you are born again, Spirit filled Christian who has been a Christian for several years, you must speak this scripture over yourself. It is not you who makes you worthy to give. It is Christ in you that has something to impart to the youth.

Matthew 28: 18 Then Jesus came and spoke to them, saying, "All authority has been given to Me in heaven and on earth. 19 Go therefore and make disciples of all nations, baptizing them in the name of the Father and of the Son and of the Holy Spirit, 20 teaching them to observe all things I have commanded you. And remember, I am with you always, even to the end of the age." Amen.

Spiritual Development

You have the authority to do it. You've received of God answers to prayers and strength to live and you know that God is Omnipotent, you've got something to give. I highly recommend that you also devote at least 3 hours a week, if possible 1-2 hours per day, to seeking God about learning spiritual things yourself. Prayer, reading the Bible, reading spiritual books, watching preaching, all things that can build you up spiritually so that you are spiritually strong and at your best also.

The more you draw from God's Spirit yourself, the more you will be able to give.

Lifelong learning commitment – continuous self-improvement

If you are using my book, you most likely want to do something to reach people but need some sort of structure to get started. My book is a flexible stricture that you can use and also write your own plans and lessons to help you mentor a youth.

Areas of strength and other areas

If there are certain things God is speaking to you in the present or impresses upon you as you are praying for the person you mentor, be sure to share those things with the person. My book is a guideline. Should God speak to you about the person, you should first obey God. You can also talk about things God has taught you. Your relationship with God is something you should talk about and share. Your unique testimony may be the very reason God has brought that youth into your life. You can witness like no other person can. Create a structure for your talks with the person.

Guidelines

As a rule, choose 3- 5 points you would like to share about the topic God places on your heart. For each of those points, include scriptures and brief testimonies to illustrate the points. Give the person a chance to comprehend what you've said. Let him or her ask questions. Assign some type of writing topic. I highly recommend the use of a journal for yourself and the student.

You keep your lessons in it as well as observations and reflection. Also, anything God speaks to you directly, place them in the book. The students should write at least 1 page on each of the lessons. The journal should be homework. The topics should be reflections on the topics you covered and on your meetings. By writing a reflection, the student will closely consider the topics and the experience. The student can later read and reread things he or she has learned and add to them. New insight will come as he or she is transformed from glory to glory by the Holy Spirit. The person should share anything he or she writes with you only as he or she feels to do it.

Life Long Learning

If you have not read any books on leadership, I would highly recommend books by John Maxwell. All of his leadership books emphasize the need for each person to enter into a professional and spiritual development process. It means you choose to give yourself to developing as a person in areas of your strength. For instance, in communication or leadership, in teaching or in management. Choose 2-3 areas to improve on and devote yourself to give at least 1 hour a day to personal development.

It could be reading a book. John Maxwell suggests reading at least 1 new book a month. It could be listening to a CD or watching a DVD. It must be related to your development in the chosen areas. What happens is that you become more excellent in all areas of your life because of the growth and stimulation. It also means you've got fresh stuff to share. You should also discuss this with your student. There are many excellent things I received in reading John Maxwell's books, but the main thing that has changed my life much is the addition of a deliberate professional development aspect into my life. The rewards are beyond what I could have imagined.

Share some of your own self-improvement plan with your student. Discuss how he or she might integrate a plan into his or her life.

Improving

Keep improving – keep a goal of improving and insert a commitment into your schedule min 1 hour day – keep it as you would any important meeting or event. Get the student to list 3-5 areas of strength. They can be topics that cover sports, business, career, serving, any spiritual gifts or natural talents. They can include personality aspects. You should do it first and if you don't have a professional development plan in place, begin it. Also teach it to the students you mentor.

2 FIRST CONTACT

Pray first

Pray as you go to church that God will direct you to a youth who desires to know more of God. Seek God by the Holy Spirit and pray for the person at least a week before you ask him or her to get together. As you see the youth in the church, let God direct you in your choice of who to invite. It could be the son or daughter of your friend. It could be a youth that has no saved family. It could be someone that God places on your heart.

The invitation

It should begin with an introduction. It can be as simple as something like "God has placed you on my heart. Please come to dinner." Or go for a coffee or invite them to lunch etc. It should be completely without any strings attached. If the person declines, you may ask a different day. If the person declines more than twice, you should let the person contact you or not persist. It is possible the person cannot come that day. If the youth does not seem interested, it is quite possible the person is not a candidate for you to connect with.

The meeting

Once the person meets with you for coffee or dinner or whatever the reason, it almost always involves some relaxing comfortable atmosphere, you can start by asking questions of the person about school or about his or her job or family. Listen carefully for any signs of distrust or disinterest or trust or interest. At the right point, mention your idea that you were praying for him or her and God placed the person on your heart with to talk to about the things of God. Directly ask the person if he is interested in knowing God in a more deliberate way. It would mean a commitment of getting together. Of course, the person could be free to quit at any time. If you are being led by the Holy Spirit, in your choices, and the person is truly seeking spiritual direction, it will fit the way a hand slips into a glove. If there is any sense of hesitation or mistrust, it isn't right and leave it at that.

You could mention that what you will do is meet either once a week for several months or once a month for 6-9 months. Approximately 2 hours commitment is necessary. You can mention about how you yourself have made a commitment or re-established a commitment to spiritual growth and that you will keep learning as long as you live. There is no Christian who has arrived. There is no perfect person. We can continue to learn about God all of this life and for all of eternity because God is beyond any human conception. His beauty and manifold nature make Him fascinating and attractive.

Philippians 3: 14 I press toward the goal to the prize of the high calling of God in Christ Jesus.

END with a decision to get together or end with the offer and wait for the reply. If the person is truly wanting God, the person will not hesitate. In my own experience, either the person is excited and wants to know when you can start or the person is all smiles and excited but needing to check his or her agenda. Also decide what would be best meeting once a month or once a week. I would suggest once a week, but it is because some busy people who would make excellent mentors may hesitate to try a once a week commitment, I have aimed for once a month. Choose the best fit for you and the youth.

Materials – Bible, pens and paper, journal – always

Always be excellent. Serve the person truly valuing him or her and caring for his or her as for Christ. Plan a snack or dinner or refreshment of some kind to give to the person each get together. Also, pray for the person daily. Purchase books, CDS, DVDS or get scriptures to sow into the person's life that will help him or her to grow. You may do it throughout the commitment as God quickens to you what things could encourage and strengthen the person.

List of Topics covered

1. Prayer
2. Praise and worship
3. Baptism of Holy Spirit – tongues
4. Using tongues to praise and worship
5. Using tongues to pray
6. Communion
7. Foot washing – men with men, women with women
8. Serving
9. Mentoring others

Sample Prayer

God I pray for the youth of our church. Give me wisdom and boldness to help disciple someone in the things of God. I do it so that the truths you have taught me may be passed on to others, so they may teach it to others also. Thank you for leading me to the right people Holy Spirit. In Jesus name. Amen.

3 HOLY SPIRIT LED LEARNING

Lesson: One

Read the scriptures or others that you prepare. Briefly discuss them

For instance, the following scripture is usually used for someone pursuing God; from glory to glory the person will be transformed. It isn't because of you; it isn't because of the person. It is the dynamic of spirit to spirit connecting with the Holy Spirit. The person will grow as he presses in to know God. It must be sincere. If it is not, nothing will occur. It is no more than a social thing. It is not negative, but it certainly is not why I am writing my book. This book is to help you guide a person through spiritual growth in the Charismatic, Pentecostal Christian Faith. It will involve the Holy Spirit. It will involve the person's human will and his spiritual desire to know God. The most important aspect is that you be lead by the Holy Spirit and you obey inner promptings to speak scriptures or to pray or to give. It is the Holy Spirit who is the teacher, teaching through you a willing vessel.

2 Corinthians 3: 17 Now the Lord is the Spirit. And where the Spirit of the Lord is, there is liberty. 18 But we all, seeing the glory of the Lord with unveiled faces, as in a mirror, are being transformed into the same image from glory to glory by the Spirit of the Lord.

This scripture is often used by people discussing financial giving, but it can also be applied to giving and learning. That is go beyond where you are right now. Plan to devote yourself to learn and apply your learning so that a year from now, you have been transformed. Give yourself wholly to God and commit yourself to the Holy Spirit's teaching and guiding.

Sample Prayer of Commitment

Holy Spirit, I commit to give myself in learning. Please prompt me, lead me, guide me. Teach me. Quicken Scriptures to me. Give me understanding, wisdom and knowledge that I may learn so that I may teach others. In Jesus name, Amen.

2 Corinthians 8: 10 And in this matter, I give my advice. It is appropriate for you, who began last year not only to give, but also to willingly give. 11 Now therefore complete the task, so that, as there was a willingness to do so, there may be a performance of it according to your means. 12 For if

there is a willing mind first, the gift is accepted according to what a man possesses and not according to what he does not possess.

Importance of passing things you have learned to others. Keep God's word as a priority. Commit yourself to the Holy Spirit to teach you.

Deuteronomy 11: 18 Therefore you must fix these words of mine in your heart and in your soul, and bind them as a sign on your hand, so that they may be as frontlets between your eyes. 19 You shall teach them to your children, speaking of them when you sit in your house and when you walk by the way, when you lie down, and when you rise up. 20 You shall write them on the doorposts of your house and on your gates, 21 so that your days and the days of your children may be multiplied in the land which the Lord swore to your fathers to give them, as long as the days of heaven on the earth.

Establish connection - relationship
Sample questions to start discussion.

Journal Topic

1. Describe for me what life is like for you at school, work, home.
2. Music listen to
3. Movies
4. Tv shows
5. Books reading or leisure activities
6. Describe your church life, commitments,
7. Hobbies and talents, sports, music, other
8. Goals for yourself for the school year or semester
9. Spiritual goals
10. Important things God has taught you
11. Instances you knew God was speaking to you or leading you
12. Instances when you knew God was using you
13. Ways you can contribute to your family, community, country
14. List spiritual gifts or any experience you directly spoke with God and you knew you were in His presence.
15. Water baptism
16. Baptized in the Holy Spirit

Keep a journal – of each meeting – also record any questions you want to discuss.

Give those questions to the student to write in his or her journal. You may choose some of the topics to discuss as the person feels free. He or she should only share what he or she feels comfortable sharing.

Start with conversation and a refreshment.

Keep it directed. Discuss the student's interests, spiritual back ground etc. Give. information about yourself.– build a relationship by sharing topics.

Give your own answers to some of the questions. Let the youth ask questions about yourself.

Discuss that you would like to present things God has taught you, so the youth can teach it to others. Explain how it is God's commandment that we teach others the things we have learned.

Give the person a journal topic. Get him to write one page about the answers to the questions above. Keeping a journal of your meetings is part of the training. A person may not remember how important something is unless it is recorded.

Always end your session with prayer. You lead the prayer but encourage the other person to pray also. Also ask if there are any prayer requests.

Example prayer

Thank you, God, for our gathering to you together day and the things we have spoken of. Let NAME THE PERSON think of things and help to direct him to excellent resources that can help him develop spiritually. God give us wisdom so that we may grow in the knowledge of God. Give us understanding. Help us to share the things we learned with others. Amen.

Gift

Give the person either a music CD of praise and worship, or a DVD of preaching or a book. Give something for the person to think about and learn from before your next meeting. If money is an issue – give scriptures for the person to read and pray about and some home-made snack or specialty.

I highly recommend that you meet either in church in a classroom or in your home with someone else home. It should in all aspects appear pure and innocent as it is. If you are married, let your spouse be present.

I highly recommend you either buy coffee and donuts or make refreshments ahead so that you can focus on the person and things of God rather than preparing something. An aspect of human life is people connect over refreshments together. It does not have to be elaborate. It can be cookies and coffee. The idea is to show the person genuine Christian hospitality.

Mentor others – relationship - invite (not one on one) to dinner or coffee.

PRAY AND PRAISE
ALWAYS RECEIVE PRAYER REQUESTS ALWAYS SERVE A SNACK
ALWAYS TALK AFTER YOUR LESSON, EVEN IF ONLY BRIEFLY

Meetings should be 1:1/2 hours -2 hours. Schedule them for 2 hours. That should include your talks, prayers, and conversation. Do not go past 2 hours. It will help you and the person to feel that it is part of your life but that it is without being a burden.

Journal topic – discuss any of the following:
Journal Topic
1. Describe for me what life is like for you at school, work, home.
2. Music listen to
3. Movies
4. Tv shows
5. Books reading or leisure activities
6. Describe your church life, commitments,
7. Hobbies and talents, sports, music, other
8. Goals for yourself for the school year or semester
9. Spiritual goals
10. Important things God has taught you
11. Instances you knew God was speaking to you or leading you
12. Instances when you knew God was using you
13. Ways you can contribute to your family, community, country
14. List spiritual gifts or any experience you directly spoke with God and you knew you were in His presence.
15. Water baptism
16. Baptized in the Holy Spirit

Keep a journal – of each meeting – also record any questions you want to discuss.

4 TRUTHS OF HEALING

Lesson 2

Establish relationship – love

Agape love – unconditional love of God

John 13: 1 Now before the Passover Feast, Jesus knew that His hour had come to depart from this world to the Father. Having loved His own who were in the world, He loved them to the end.

Luke 6: 38 Give, and it will be given to you: Good measure, pressed down, shaken together, and running over will men give unto you. For with the measure you use, it will be measured unto you."

Share what you have learned. 3-5 points God has taught you - briefly discuss

1. Salvation
2. Healing and/ or deliverance
3. Being prompted by the Holy Spirit

Write 3-5 important things– get the person to tell you about his or her relationship with God. Listen carefully for clues of revelation or of desire to learn more.

2 Timothy 2: 2 So you, my son, be strong in the grace that is in Christ Jesus. 2 Share the things that you have heard from me in the presence of many witnesses with faithful men who will be able to teach others also.

Give books or CDS or DVDs –

Buy books CD's, DVDs – try to sow spiritually into the person's life over the duration of the gathering. The duration of the mentoring should be at least 6 months – 9 Months for approximately 2 hours. You could get the duration shorter by meeting once a week for several months.

Discussion/ Journal Topics
•   What do you want from God? Be specific personal, career, family,

friends. life characteristics and things, you've done you would want to leave as a legacy

Examine your own heart

Talk and write about your relationship with God. Describe your relationship.

3-5 areas – get the candidate to discuss – also to write it in his journal.

2 Corinthians 2: 5 Examine yourselves, seeing whether you are in the faith; test yourselves. Do you not know that Jesus Christ is in you? unless indeed you are disqualified.

Journal question

1.Ask person questions about – areas of strength, areas of interest in scripture, personal spiritual growth plan, friends, listing to what types of music – reading what types of books – LISTEN

Find out if the person is interested in getting together with you as a mentor Encourage spiritual growth

Areas of growth in God – prayer, faith, praise, relationship, evangelism, spiritual gifts

Requirements for the dedication to Holy Spirit Leaning:
Persistence
Conviction
Faith

Journal can include discussion of

1.   Salvation
2.   Healing and/ or deliverance
3.   Being prompted by the Holy Spirit

Healing

Healing of Blind Bartimaeus Mark 10 : 46 Then they came to Jericho. And as He went out of Jericho with His disciples and a great number of people, blind Bartimaeus, the son of Timaeus, sat along the way begging. 47 When he heard that it was Jesus of Nazareth, he began to cry out, "Jesus, Son of

David, have mercy on me!"

48 Many ordered him to keep silent. But he cried out even more, "Son of David, have mercy on me!"

49 Jesus stood still and commanded him to be called.

So they called the blind man, saying, "Be of good comfort. Rise, He is calling you." 50 Throwing aside his garment, he rose and came to Jesus.

51 Jesus answered him, "What do you want Me to do for you?"

The blind man said to Him, "Rabbi, that I might receive my sight."

52 Jesus said to him, "Go your way. Your faith has made you well." Immediately he received his sight and followed Jesus on the way.

Life point – God will give you what you want if you seek Him with all your being.

2.next visit – goals for school, career, life, relationships, school year, job, Listen – these should be written someplace. If they are not, have the person write it in his or her journal.

3. invest in them by showing them the way. Read scripture – talk about it. Pray about it together

4. Any service within the church you do – invite him or her to help

Your meetings should be in your home or church or in a quiet spot.

You are connected in the Body of Christ

Explain the Scriptures

It is God's desire to heal. Pray for any people needing healing. Begin to intercede or pray for others as part of your regular prayer life.

Give Yourself wholly to God

Romans 12: 1 I urge you therefore, brothers, by the mercies of God, that you present your bodies as a living sacrifice, holy, and acceptable to God, which is your reasonable service of worship. 2 Do not be conformed to this world, but be transformed by the renewing of your mind, that you may prove what is the good and acceptable and perfect will of God.

Prayer: Before you start prayer, ask the Holy Spirit to place people on your heart who you should be praying for.

ALWAYS RECEIVE PRAYER REQUESTS ALWAYS SERVE A SNACK
ALWAYS TALK AFTER YOUR LESSON, EVEN IF ONLY BRIEFLY

Journal Question – write approximately 1 page

1. Salvation
2. Healing and/ or deliverance
3. Being prompted by the Holy Spirit

Discuss your point of view of the get togthers. Explain anything you have learned through them or anything God is placing on your heart.

5 COMMUNION

Lesson 3

Start with praise and worship and the new song of the LORD.

If the person does not know how to use the new song of the LORD, explain it to him. Get him to praise God in his own words. It simply means worshipping God by saying or singing His glory and holiness and what He has done for your life.

Communion

Explain how communion was used in the home of the early church as they daily gathered.

Read and explain the scripture.
- Got teaching from the Apostles and lived by it
- Continued with communion and dinners together
- They shared their finances so no one did without
- They met daily – communion and prayer
- They were praising God
- God continued to bless and prosper them

Acts 2: 42 They continued steadfastly in the apostles' teaching and fellowship, in the breaking of bread and in the prayers. 43 Fear came to every soul. And many wonders and signs were done through the apostles. 44 All who believed were together and had all things in common. 45 They sold their property and goods and distributed them to all, according to their need. 46 And continuing daily with one mind in the temple, and breaking bread from house to house, they ate their food with gladness and simplicity of heart, 47 praising God and having favor with all the people. And the Lord added to the church daily those who were being saved.

Explain it was in direct obedience to Jesus who commanded us to do these things.

Communion - Get the person to take part in serving communion
Give yourself to God as an offering – worship

Romans 12:1-2 Romans 12: 12 I urge you therefore, brothers, by the mercies of God, that you present your bodies as a living sacrifice, holy, and acceptable to God, which is your reasonable service of worship. 2 Do not be conformed to this world, but be transformed by the renewing of your mind, that you may prove what is the good and acceptable and perfect will of God.

Wholly spirit soul body – 1 Thessalonians 5: 23 May the very God of peace sanctify you completely. And I pray to God that your whole spirit, soul, and body be preserved blameless unto the coming of our Lord Jesus Christ.

Read the scriptures.
Points for communion:
Quoting directly what Jesus said – Jesus body given as a sacrifice
Jesus blood given as a sacrifice

With faith – we partake – death, burial, resurrection of Jesus Christ by faith Important – to keep heart right with God – examine your own heart Pray the Holy Spirit will quicken to you – not a ritual = it is a sacrament

1 Corinthians 11: 23 I have received of the Lord that which I delivered to you: that the Lord Jesus, on the night in which He was betrayed, took bread. 24 When He had given thanks, He broke it and said, "Take and eat. This is My body which is broken for you. Do this in remembrance of Me."[a] 25 In the same manner He took the cup after He had supper, saying, "This cup is the new covenant in My blood. Do this, as often as you drink it, in remembrance of Me."[b] 26 As often as you eat this bread and drink this cup, you proclaim the Lord's death until He comes.

John 6: 30 Therefore they said to Him, "What sign do You show then, that we may see and believe You? What work will You perform? 31 Our fathers ate manna in the desert. As it is written, 'He gave them bread from heaven to eat.'[c]"

32 Then Jesus said, "Truly, truly I say to you, Moses did not give you the bread from heaven, but My Father gives you the true bread from heaven. 33 For the bread of God is He who comes down from heaven and gives life to the world."

34 Then they said to Him, "Lord, give us this bread always."

35 Jesus said to them, "I am the bread of life. Whoever comes to Me shall never hunger, and whoever believes in Me shall never thirst. 36 But I told you that you have seen Me, and yet do not believe. 37 All whom the Father gives Me will come to Me, and he who comes to Me I will never cast out. 38 For I came down from heaven, not to do My own will, but the will of Him who sent Me. 39 This is the will of the Father who has sent Me, that of all whom He has given Me, I should lose nothing, but should raise it up at the last day. 40 This is the will of Him who sent Me, that everyone who sees the Son and believes in Him may have eternal life, and I will raise him up on the last day."

41 The Jews then murmured about Him, because He said, "I am the bread which came down from heaven." 42 They said, "Is this not Jesus, the son of Joseph, whose father and mother we know? How is it then that He says, 'I have come down from heaven'? "

43 Jesus therefore answered them, "Do not murmur among yourselves. 44 No one can come to Me unless the Father who has sent Me draws him. And I will raise him up on the last day. 45 It is written in the Prophets, 'They shall all be taught by God.'[d] Therefore everyone who has heard and has learned of the Father comes to Me. 46 Not that anyone has seen the Father, except He who is from God. He has seen the Father. 47 Truly, truly I say to you, whoever believes in Me has eternal life. 48 I am the bread of life. 49 Your fathers ate manna in the wilderness, and they died. 50 This is the bread which comes down from heaven, that one may eat of it and not die. 51 I am the living bread which came down from heaven. If anyone eats of this bread, he will live forever. The bread which I shall give for the life of the world is My flesh."

52 The Jews therefore quarreled among themselves, saying, "How can this Man give us His flesh to eat?"

53 Jesus said to them, "Truly, truly I say to you, unless you eat the flesh of the Son of Man and drink His blood, you have no life in you. 54 Whoever eats My flesh and drinks My blood has eternal life. And I will raise him up on the last day. 55 For My flesh is food indeed, and My blood is drink indeed. 56 Whoever eats My flesh and drinks My blood remains in Me, and I in him. 57 As the living Father sent Me, and I live because of the Father, so whoever feeds on Me also will live because of Me. 58 This is the bread which came down from heaven, not as your fathers ate manna and died. He who eats this bread will live forever." 59 He said these things in the synagogue, as He taught in Capernaum.

61 Knowing in Himself that His disciples murmured about it, Jesus said to them, "Does this offend you? 62 Then what if you see the Son of Man ascend to where He was before? 63 It is the Spirit who gives life. The flesh profits nothing. The words that I speak to you are spirit and are life. 64 But there are some of you who do not believe." For Jesus knew from the beginning who they were who did not believe, and who it was who would betray Him. 65 Then He said, "For this reason I have said to you that no one can come to Me unless it were given him by My Father."

Important

To lightly take communion is as though you are abusing Jesus
It must be a sober, self-giving to God

Hold the bread and pray thanking Jesus for giving His life for you.
Hold the cup of juice or wine. Pray thanking Jesus for His blood shed for you. Give thanks to God for the blessings of the new covenant.

Partaking of the Supper Unworthily

1 Corinthians 11: 27 Therefore whoever eats this bread and drinks this cup of the Lord unworthily will be guilty of the body and blood of the Lord. 28 Let a man examine himself, and so eat of the bread and drink of the cup. 29 For he who eats and drinks unworthily, eats and drinks damnation to himself, not discerning the Lord's body. 30 For this reason many are weak and unhealthy among you, and many die. 31 If we would judge ourselves, we would not be judged. 32 But when we are judged, we are disciplined by the Lord, so that we would not be condemned with the world.

33 So, my brothers, when you come together to eat, wait for one another. 34 If anyone hungers, let him eat at home, so that you may not come together into condemnation.

I will set the rest in order when I come.

Prepare 2-3 worship songs – either on a cd or play the music. If not acapella is ok. Thank God praise God for the new covenant.

PRAY AND PRAISE
ALWAYS RECEIVE PRAYER REQUESTS ALWAYS SERVE A SNACK
ALWAYS TALK AFTER YOUR LESSON, EVEN IF ONLY BRIEFLY

Journal Question

Explain any revelation you have concerning communion. Explain the significance of keeping Communion. Write about what God is teaching you and any aspect of your relationship with Him.

6 SPIRITUAL DESIRE

Lesson 4

How much of God do you want?
God will never force you. He will draw you unto Himself. You can obey or not. Your choice determines your life.
Isiah 55: 6 Seek the Lord while He may be found,
    call you upon Him while He is near.

Intimacy with God
Key points for the scriptures.

Like comparing God to a deep river.
Ankles – casual relationship
Knees – some type of commitment
Loins - You are giving yourself to God mostly
Depths - You have completely given your life to God and are living in the Spirit each day.

River is as the Holy Spirit of God –

Explain the scriptures on levels of giving yourself to God.

Ezekiel 47: 3 When the man who had the line in his hand went eastward, he measured a thousand cubits, and he brought me through the water; the water reached the ankles. 4 Again he measured a thousand and brought me through the water. The water reached the knees. Again he measured a thousand and brought me through the water. The water reached the loins. 5 Afterward he measured a thousand. And it was a river that I could not pass over, for the water had risen, enough water to swim in, a river that could not be passed over. 6 He said to me, "Son of man, have you seen this?"

Then he brought me and caused me to return to the brink of the river. 7 When I had returned I saw on the bank of the river very many trees on the one side and on the other. 8 Then he said to me, "This water flows toward the eastern region and goes down into the valley, and enters the sea. When it flows into the sea, the water will become fresh. 9 Every living creature that swarms, wherever the rivers go, will live. And there shall be a very great multitude of fish, because these waters shall come there and the others become fresh. Thus everything shall live wherever the river comes. 10 It shall come to pass that the fishermen shall stand upon it. From En Gedi even to En Eglaim there shall be a place to spread out nets. Their fish shall be according to their kinds, as the fish of the Mediterranean Sea, exceedingly many. 11 But its miry places and its marshes shall not be healed. They shall be given to salt. 12 By the river upon its bank, on this side and on that side, shall grow all kinds of trees for food, whose leaf shall not fade nor shall its fruit fail. They shall bring forth fruit according to their months, because their water issues out of the sanctuary. And their fruit shall be for food and their leaves for medicine."

Aim to grow in relationship with God. Prayer, praise, self-improvement, Bible study – integrate into your life.

PRAY OVER THE SCRIPTURE AND LET THE HOLY SPIRIT DIRECT YOUR PRAYER

SAMPLE PRAYER

O Holy Spirit,
I thank you that you dwell inside of me. Thank you for my life and for new life in the Spirit springing up on the inside of me. Come fill me to overflowing. O God, I desire you. Fill me with your holy presence so that I may know you beyond what I have known. I desire your manifest presence. The height, the width, the depth, the breadth of your love for me is beyond what I can comprehend. Fill me with your presence. I worship you Jesus…Begin to praise and worship God.

Sample prayer

O God, as , NAME OF STUDENT, gives himself or herself to you wholly, fill him or her to overflowing with the Holy Spirit.Let him or desire you more than anything else. Draw him or her closer to know you deeper. . ENCOURGE THE PERON TO PRAY AND PRAISE GOD WITH THE NEW SONG.

Praise and worship

Sing 3-5 choruses or songs. Provide the words. Try to get a musician to be there who can lead worship. If not, you lead the worship. Pray for an atmosphere of the Holy Spirit's presence. If the person is baptized in the Holy Spirit, encourage him or her to worship God in tongues.. If he or she has not been baptized in the Holy Spirit, get the person to praise God with the new song – praising and thanking God for personal things. If you praise or pray in tongues, explain it to the person quoting Acts 2.

Acts 2: 38 Peter said to them, "Repent and be baptized, every one of you, in the name of Jesus Christ for the forgiveness of sins, and you shall receive the gift of the Holy Spirit. 39 For the promise is to you, and to your children, and to all who are far away, as many as the Lord our God will call."

The Baptism of the Holy Spirit is promised to all believers. If the person is not baptized in the Holy Spirit explain that he or she can be. (leave it there). If the person is baptized in the Holy Spirit pray and praise in tongues together thanking God for the Holy Spirit.

PRAY AND PRAISE
ALWAYS RECEIVE PRAYER REQUESTS ALWAYS SERVE A SNACK
ALWAYS TALK AFTER YOUR LESSON, EVEN IF ONLY BRIEFLY

Journal Topic – explain how important is praise and worship to your life and if you regularly include it in your daily relationship with God. Explain your impression of today's get together on the topic of giving yourself to God wholly.

7. BAPTISM OF THE HOLY SPIRIT

Lesson 5
TEACH – also invite a musician or worship leader or you lead worship.

Get him to give details of his salvation.
Find out about water baptism, baptism of the Holy Spirit
If you have not already discuss it – also give your own experience and how it has changed your life.

Points to cover
- They prayed for the Holy Spirit because Jesus told them to wait for it
- God's Holy Spirit filled them
- They were speaking in other languages they hadn't learned
- It compelled them to go into the street
- They were worshipping and praising God
- It gave them boldness to witness
- Peter preached salvation and over 2000 people were saved and baptized
- Empowering presence of Holy Spirit to be a witness for God – to equip you
-

Acts 2: 2 Suddenly a sound like a mighty rushing wind came from heaven, and it filled the whole house where they were sitting. 3 There appeared to them tongues as of fire, being distributed and resting on each of them, 4 and they were all filled with the Holy Spirit and began to speak in other tongues, as the Spirit enabled them to speak.

Luke 24: 45 Then He opened their minds to understand the Scriptures. 46 He said to them, "Thus it is written, and accordingly it was necessary for the Christ to suffer and to rise from the dead the third day, 47 and that repentance and remission of sins should be preached in His name to all nations, beginning at Jerusalem. 48 You are witnesses of these things. 49 And look, I am sending the promise of My Father upon you. But wait in the city of Jerusalem until you are clothed with power from on high."

John 14: 15 "If you love Me, keep My commandments. 16 I will pray the Father, and He will give you another Counselor, that He may be with you forever: 17 the Spirit of truth, whom the world cannot receive, for it does not see Him, neither does it know Him. But you know Him, for He lives with you, and will be in you. 18 I will not leave you fatherless. I will come to you. 19 Yet a little while and the world will see Me no more. But you will see Me. Because I live, you will live also. 20 On that day you will know that

I am in My Father, and you are in Me, and I am in you. 21 He who has My commandments and keeps them is the one who loves Me. And he who loves Me will be loved by My Father. And I will love him and will reveal Myself to him."

Acts 19: 1 While Apollos was at Corinth, Paul passed through the upper regions and came to Ephesus. He found some disciples 2 and said to them, "Have you received the Holy Spirit since you believed?"

They said to him, "No, we have not even heard that there is a Holy Spirit."

3 He said to them, "Into what then were you baptized?"

They said, "Into John's baptism."

4 Paul said, "John indeed baptized with the baptism of repentance, telling the people that they should believe in the One coming after him, that is, in Christ Jesus." 5 When they heard this, they were baptized in the name of the Lord Jesus. 6 When Paul had laid his hands on them, the Holy Spirit came on them, and they spoke in other tongues and prophesied. 7 There were about twelve men in all.

Holy Spirit baptism is a promise to all who believe.

As in last week's lesson we discussed how much of God you desire – you've got to want more of God to get the Baptism of the Holy Spirit. He will give it to you. It is his promise.

Acts 2: 38 Peter said to them, "Repent and be baptized, every one of you, in the name of Jesus Christ for the forgiveness of sins, and you shall receive the gift of the Holy Spirit. 39 For the promise is to you, and to your children, and to all who are far away, as many as the Lord our God will call."

You know it is a gift from God.

God will not force you – should you truly want more of God and want Him to fill you with Him presence to overflowing, simply with all your heart – ask that you might receive it.
Worship is often the best place to begin. Praise and worship God. Start praising God with the new song of God. Keep worshipping once you have asked God for the gift.

As words come to you – speak them. You must do the speaking. You must speak them.

God may give you a song or a phrase. Repeat it as a prayer unto Him.

Prepare some songs 3- 5 to sing to use to invite the Holy Spirit to come and to be as a starting point for praise and worship. It is in the atmosphere of praise and worship most people are baptized in the Holy Spirit.

PRAISE AND WORSHIP – PLAY AN INSTRUMENT OR INVITE SOMEONE WHO CAN LEAD WORSHIP. You could play a praise and worship CD and print the words and sing along with it. The Importance is on worshipping God and releasing faith for the Baptism of the Holy Spirit.

Explain you will pray for the person to be filled with the Holy Spirit. If the person does not want it, do not do it. If the person agrees, continue. PRAY FOR IMPARTATION OF THE BAPTISM OF THE HOLY SPIRIT

As you see the person worshipping, as the Holy Spirit leads, place your hands on the person's head or shoulders believing in faith God will use you.

Sample prayer

O Jesus

NAME HIM OR HER, wants a fresh touch of the Holy Spirit. God, you promised to baptize us in the Holy Spirit if we believe. I pray the impartation of the Holy Spirit to overflow in NAME person's life. Baptize him or her in the Name of Jesus Christ. Be filled with the Holy Spirit to overflowing.

Start praising God with the new song of God.
Continue praising God with the new song of God.

IF THE PERSON IS BAPTIZED IN THE HOLY SPIRIT, EXPLAIN IMPORTANCE OF REGLARILY PRAYING IN THE SPIRIT AND WORSHIPPING IN THE SPIRIT.

It builds faith and strengthens the inner man.
It lets you follow the leading of the Holy Spirit to pray for you and through you.

Jude 1: 20 But you, beloved, build yourselves up in your most holy faith. Pray in the Holy Spirit. 21 Keep yourselves in the love of God while you are waiting for the mercy of our Lord Jesus Christ, which leads to eternal life.

Ephesians 5: 19 Speak to one another in psalms, hymns, and spiritual songs, singing and making melody in your heart to the Lord. 20 Give thanks always for all things to God the Father in the name of our Lord Jesus Christ, 21 being submissive to one another in the fear of God.

If you have a certain phrase God has given you, as you are praising use it. Keep praying it until you get another one. Continue to praise God in the prayer language God gives you. Expect God to give you new words and phrases.

Praying in the Holy Spirit is God the Holy Spirit praying in you and through you the perfect will of God for you and others.

Romans 8: 26 Likewise, the Spirit helps us in our weaknesses, for we do not know what to pray for as we ought, but the Spirit Himself intercedes for us with groanings too deep for words. 27 He who searches the hearts knows what the mind of the Spirit is, because He intercedes for the saints according to the will of God.

God wants to use us in prayer and praise but also in witnessing to people.

Importance of words we hear and words we speak
LET THE WORDS OF MY MOUTH

Psalm 19: 14 Let the words of my mouth and the meditation of my heart
   be acceptable in Your sight,
   O Lord, my strength and my Redeemer.

SET A GUARD OVER MY MOUTH

Psalm 141: 3 Set a guard, O Lord, over my mouth;
   keep watch over the door of my lips.

GETTING OUR WORDS IN ALIGNMENT WITH WHAT GOD SAYS ABOUT US.

6. praising – worship – using the gift of tongues to worship and also to pray – SHOULD BE IN PRIVATE PLACE – QUIET PLACE - FREEDOM

PSALM 100

Psalm 100
A Psalm of thanksgiving.
1 Make a joyful noise unto the Lord, all the earth!
2   Serve the Lord with gladness;
    come before His presence with singing.
3 Know that the Lord, He is God;
    it is He who has made us, and not we ourselves;
    we are His people, and the sheep of His pasture.
4 Enter into His gates with thanksgiving,
    and into His courts with praise;
    be thankful to Him, and bless His name.
5 For the Lord is good; His mercy endures forever,
    and His faithfulness to all generations.

PSALM 150

1 Praise the Lord!
 Praise God in His sanctuary;
    praise Him in the firmament of His power!
2 Praise Him for His mighty acts;
    praise Him according to His excellent greatness!
3 Praise Him with the sound of the trumpet;
    praise Him with the lyre and harp!
4 Praise Him with the tambourine and dancing;
    praise Him with stringed instruments and flute!
5 Praise Him with loud cymbals;
    praise Him with the clanging cymbals!
6 Let everything that has breath praise the Lord.
 Praise the Lord!

Sample Conclusion prayer

Thank you for baptizing or the fresh infilling of the Spirit over NAME'S life. Thank you, O God for opportunities to praise and worship you in the future. Cleanse our mouths that we might speak truth and witness with boldness for Christ. Amen.

Find out what type of praise and worship they are listening to.

Introduce a Christian CD or digital music. Worship

Literally sing worship and praise songs together and flow in the new song of the LORD – praising God in your own words – encourage them to do the same. Do it each occasion you get together from that day on.

Discuss the journal topic together OR

Option: Watch a Christian concert or DVD.

Music is a normal way people enjoy their leisure. Many people listen to music that is not pleasing to God and that does not encourage or build up his or her spirit. – Delicately, explain that whatever you sow into your being you will reap from it. That means you are affected by the music you listen to.

Music, movies, television are more than entertainment. They are inputs into your spirit man. These things can build you up spiritually or sow unbelief, fear and strife into your heart.

Pray – Gently lead the person in prayer–Let the Holy Spirit bring conviction if the person is listening to things or watching things he or she should not. – Pray that God will truly reveal the truth about music movies and other forms of leisure activity.

PRAY AND PRAISE
ALWAYS RECEIVE PRAYER REQUESTS ALWAYS SERVE A SNACK
ALWAYS TALK AFTER YOUR LESSON, EVEN IF ONLY BRIEFLY

Journal Topic

Discussion of importance of the Baptism of the Holy Spirit. Explain the experience and how it helps you to witness. Each day during the week, pray and or praise in tongues so that you not only praise God but build up your spirit.

8 COVENANT GOD

Lesson 6
Review covenants of God – Covenant God made with man.
Use scriptures in the Bible.

covenant – discuss Abraham, Moses, Noah, Jesus

Abraham
- Circumcision of the males
- God would bless those who bless them and fight against those who fight against them
- Promise made by God; it is always true.
-

Abraham – 17: Then God said to Abraham, "As for you, you shall keep My covenant, you and your descendants after you throughout their generations. 10 This is My covenant, which you shall keep, between Me and you and your descendants after you; every male among you shall be circumcised. 11 You shall circumcise the flesh of your foreskins, and it shall be a sign of the covenant between Me and you. 12 Every male throughout every generation that is eight days old shall be circumcised, whether born in your household or bought with money from a foreigner who is not your descendant. 13 He who is born in your house and he who is bought with your money must be circumcised. My covenant shall be in your flesh as an everlasting covenant. 14 Any uncircumcised male whose flesh of his foreskin is not circumcised shall be cut off from his people. He has broken My covenant."

Noah
Points to discuss -
Command to build an ark
Promise kept as they were saved from flood
Rainbow in the cloud to show God's covenant
God would never destroy all people and animals again as long as earth remains
God would bless them to multiply

Noah – Genesis 9: 8 Again God spoke to Noah and to his sons with him, saying, 9 "As for Me, I establish My covenant with you, and with your descendants after you; 10 and with every living creature that is with you, the birds, the livestock, and every beast of the earth with you; of all that comes out of the ark, every beast of the earth. 11 I establish My covenant with you. Never again shall all flesh be cut off by the waters of a flood. Never again shall there be a flood to destroy the earth."

12 Then God said, "This is the sign of the covenant which I am making between Me and you and every living creature that is with you, for all future generations. 13 I have set My rainbow in the cloud, and it shall be a sign of a covenant between Me and the earth. 14 When I bring a cloud over the earth, the rainbow will be seen in the cloud; 15 then I will remember My covenant, which is between Me and you and every living creature of all flesh, and the waters will never again become a flood to destroy all flesh. 16 The rainbow will appear in the cloud, and I will see it and remember the everlasting covenant between God and every living creature of all flesh that is on the earth."

17 So God said to Noah, "This is the sign of the covenant that I have established between Me and all flesh that is on the earth."

Moses
Points to discuss

God promised to deliver Israel out of bondage in Egypt
God kept His word – miracles and wonders
God had Moses bring the people to Mt Sinai
Moses obeyed
The commandments were given
Also, other Levitical laws were given
Commandments are God's will for people – pleasing to God and to show love towards people.
Keeping the commandments means God would bless them in all their lives.
Disobeying the commandments could mean punishment or death.

Moses - Exodus 20: 1 Now God spoke all these words, saying:

2 I am the Lord your God, who brought you out of the land of Egypt, out of the house of bondage.

3 You shall have no other gods before Me.

4 You shall not make for yourself any graven idol, or any likeness of anything that is in heaven above, or that is in the earth beneath, or that is in the water below the earth. 5 You shall not bow down to them or serve them; for I, the Lord your God, am a jealous God, visiting the iniquity of the fathers on the children to the third and fourth generation of them who hate Me, 6 and showing lovingkindness to thousands of them who love Me

and keep My commandments.

7 You shall not take the name of the Lord your God in vain, for the Lord will not hold guiltless anyone who takes His name in vain.

8 Remember the Sabbath day and keep it holy. 9 Six days you shall labor and do all your work, 10 but the seventh day is a Sabbath to the Lord your God. On it you shall not do any work, you, or your son, or your daughter, or your male servant, or your female servant, or your livestock, or your sojourner who is within your gates. 11 For in six days the Lord made heaven and earth, the sea, and all that is in them, and rested on the seventh day. Therefore the Lord blessed the Sabbath day and made it holy.

12 Honor your father and your mother, that your days may be long in the land which the Lord your God is giving you.

13 You shall not murder.

14 You shall not commit adultery.

15 You shall not steal.

16 You shall not bear false witness against your neighbor.

17 You shall not covet your neighbor's house; you shall not covet your neighbor's wife, or his manservant, or his maidservant, or his ox, or his donkey, or anything that is your neighbor's.
8. Get the person to participate in reading the Bible and sharing the meaning
Read the scripture – pray for revelation – talk about it

Jesus covenant with us is eternal.
Jesus fulfilled all the requirements of Messiah so He could be our Saviour..
Faith in Jesus gives us the inheritance of Abraham and the Mosaic Covenant.

As time permits - include communion

Communion

- Jesus fulfilled all the prophecies of the Messiah promised to Israel.
- Jesus gave his life as a sacrifice for those who would believe
- Communion is a sacrament – a way to keep remembrance of what

God did.

- Blessings of the New covenant include all the promises of the Mosaic covenant and the promises to Abraham and Moses.
- Includes eternal life with promise Jesus is coming back again
- Thank God for His covenant with you; give yourself in covenant to God.

Matthew 26: 26 As they were eating, Jesus took bread, blessed it and broke it, and gave it to the disciples and said, "Take and eat. This is My body."

27 Then He took the cup, and after He gave thanks, He gave it to them, saying, "Drink of it, all of you. 28 For this is My blood of the new covenant, which is shed for many for the remission of sins. 29 I say to you, I will not drink of this fruit of the vine from now on until that day when I drink it new with you in My Father's kingdom."

30 And when they had sung a hymn, they went out to the Mount of Olives.

PRAY AND PRAISE
ALWAYS RECEIVE PRAYER REQUESTS ALWAYS SERVE A SNACK
ALWAYS TALK AFTER YOUR LESSON, EVEN IF ONLY BRIEFLY

Journal Topic
Explain what you understand to be the most important aspects of covenant with Jesus. Explain what he offers and what you offer.

9 FOOTWASHING

Lesson 7   Serving: teaching by doing

You will require warm water, Lysol or disinfectant, towels.

1.Read the scriptures on foot washing. First.

9. Servant leadership – Foot washing
Jesus served us – He humbled himself as a servant

Phil. 2: 5 Let this mind be in you all, which was also in Christ Jesus,
 6 who, being in the form of God,
    did not consider equality with God something to be grasped.
7 But He emptied Himself,
    taking upon Himself the form of a servant,
    and was made in the likeness of men.
8 And being found in the form of a man,
    He humbled Himself
    and became obedient to death,
        even death on a cross.
9 Therefore God highly exalted Him
    and gave Him the name which is above every name,
10 that at the name of Jesus every knee should bow,
    of those in heaven and on earth and under the earth,
11 and every tongue should confess that Jesus Christ is Lord,
    to the glory of God the Father.[a]

The sacrament of foot washing
Pray over the person blessings
Pray over the person a scripture

John 13: 12 So when He had washed their feet, and put on His garments, and sat down again, He said to them, "Do you know what I have done to you? 13 You call Me Teacher and Lord. You speak accurately, for so I am. 14 If I then, your Lord and Teacher, have washed your feet, you also ought to wash one another's feet. 15 For I have given you an example, that you should do as I have done to you. 16 Truly, truly I say to you, a servant is not greater than his master, nor is he who is sent greater than he who sent him. 17 If you know these things, blessed are you if you do them.

Emphasize serving - doing all as unto Colossians 3: 23 And whatever you do, do it heartily, as for the Lord and not for men, 24 knowing that from the Lord you will receive the reward of the inheritance. For you serve the Lord Christ.

Ephesians 6: 5 Servants, obey those who are your masters according to the flesh, with fear and trembling, in sincerity of your heart, as to Christ, 6 not serving when eyes are on you, but as pleasing men as the servants of Christ, doing the will of God from the heart, 7 with good will doing service, as to the Lord, and not to men, 8 knowing that whatever good thing any man does, he will receive the same from the Lord, whether he is enslaved or free.

Emphasize Giving
As you are giving and serving others, God uses you to accomplish much.

2 Corinthians 9: 6 But this I say: He who sows sparingly will also reap sparingly, and he who sows bountifully will also reap bountifully. 7 Let every man give according to the purposes in his heart, not grudgingly or out of necessity, for God loves a cheerful giver. 8 God is able to make all grace abound toward you, so that you, always having enough of everything, may abound to every good work.

1 Corinthians 10: 31 Therefore, whether you eat, or drink, or whatever you do, do it all to the glory of God.

Colossians 3: 17 And whatever you do in word or deed, do all in the name of the Lord Jesus, giving thanks to God the Father through Him.

After the lesson,

GET A BASIN WITH WARM WATER AND DISINFECTANT.
KNEEL AT THE PERSON'S FEET AFTER HE REMOVES HIS SHOES. PLACE THE WATER OVER HIS FEET AND PRAY THAT GOD WILL BLESS HIM. PRAY SCRIPTURES AND BLESSINGS.

SCRIPTURES – YOU SHOULD PREPARE SOME BEOFRE THE MEETING – 2 or 3 to pray over the person. You should write them or type them and give them to him also.

Sample Scriptures
Pray scriptures of blessing over the student.

2 Corinthians 3: 18 But we all, seeing the glory of the Lord with unveiled faces, as in a mirror, are being transformed into the same image from glory to glory by the Spirit of the Lord.

Isaiah 61: 3B that they might be called trees of righteousness,
    the planting of the Lord,
    that He might be glorified.

Psalm 37: 3 Trust in the Lord, and do good;
    dwell in the land, and practice faithfulness.
4 Delight yourself in the Lord,
    and He will give you the desires of your heart.

PRAY AS GOD DIRECTS YOU – IT SHOULD BE MEANIGFUL – THAT MEANS NOT CASUAL, BUT ON PURPOSE. YOU COULD TELL THE PERSON TO WORSHIP GOD AS YOU PRAY BLESSINGS ON HIM OR HER.

AFTERWARDS, TAKE EACH FOOT AND DRY IT WITH A TOWEL UNTIL IT IS COMPLETELY DRY.

Often this humbling experience draws tears from both the giver and the receiver. GIVE THE PERSON THE OPPORTUNITY TO WASH YOUR FEET AND PRAY BLESSINGS ON YOU. YOU MUST INCLUDE THIS PART. IF THE PERSON DOESN'T DO IT, IT WILL BE INCOMPLETE. THE HUMILITY OF CHRIST IS OUR MODEL. YOU CAN HELP THE PERSON BY DIRECTING HIM IF HE DOESN'T KNOW WHAT TO DO. Encourage him or her to worship God as you are praying for him or her. Encourage him or her to pray over you letting the Holy Spirit lead him or her as he or she is washing your feet.

IF YOU SERVE IN THE CHURCH, INVITE THE PERSON TO HELP YOU

ENCOURAGE THE YOUTH TO JOIN IN VOLUNTEERING IN THE CHURCH

PRAY AND PRAISE
ALWAYS RECEIVE PRAYER REQUESTS ALWAYS SERVE A

SNACK
ALWAYS TALK AFTER YOUR LESSON, EVEN IF ONLY BRIEFLY

You may discuss the journal topic or topic of your choice.

Journal Topic: describe the importance of foot washing as taught in the scriptures. Explain areas you serve or volunteer in church or areas you are interested in volunteering.

.

10 GOD'S WORD

Lesson 8
Importance of God's Word in our lives daily.

God gave commandments to Moses. Israel instructed to know them, to obey them and to live by them.

Points to cover about reading and praying the scriptures

Emphasized to Joshua upon entering the promised land.
Emphasized to us today because God's Word is His will for us. It is essential that we put the word as the first priority in our lives.
Reason is God's ways for us are clearly written in his word. He shows us what things we aught to do doing, and what things we should not do. He shows us what things we should develop and what things to cut off. God's Word is as a mighty sword that divides right from wrong.
God's Word teaches us. Read God's Word prayerfully.
God's word aligns us with God's will.
We must read the word, study the word, pray the word, confess the Word. The Word will become so much a part of you that it will become your first response. You will be as God's Holy people – a covenant people. God will give us wisdom from His Word. It can help us with all aspects of life.

Psalm 119 – much emphasis on the importance of God's Word. I highly recommend that you read it in a translation that you can understand. Proverbs has much wisdom within them. Reading them over and praying them will help you to live your life.

God's Word is a divider – like a sword.

Hebrews 4: 12 For the word of God is alive, and active, and sharper than any two-edged sword, piercing even to the division of soul and spirit, of joints and marrow, and able to judge the thoughts and intents of the heart. 13 There is no creature that is not revealed in His sight, for all things are bare and exposed to the eyes of Him to whom we must give account.

Joshua instructed to keep importance of the Word of God.

Joshua 1: 7 Be strong and very courageous, in order to act carefully in accordance with all the law that My servant Moses commanded you. Do not turn aside from it to the right or the left, so that you may succeed wherever you go. 8 This Book of the Law must not depart from your mouth. Meditate on it day and night so that you may act carefully according to all that is written in it. For then you will make your way successful, and you will be wise. 9 Have not I commanded you? Be strong and courageous. Do not be afraid or dismayed, for the Lord your God is with you wherever you go."

Faith comes by hearing and hearing comes by the Word of God. The Word of God has within itself the ability to bring itself to come to pass. The Word of God releases faith .

Romans 10: 17 So then faith comes by hearing, and hearing by the word of God.

It means you must read the word, pray the word and confess the word to align yourself with God's Word. If you were not raised in a Christian home, it will be a new way of living for you.

God's Word is always right.

Psalm 19:
7 The law of the Lord is perfect,
    converting the soul;
the testimony of the Lord is sure,
    making wise the simple;
8 the statutes of the Lord are right,
    rejoicing the heart;
the commandment of the Lord is pure,
    enlightening the eyes;
9 the fear of the Lord is clean,
    enduring forever;
the judgments of the Lord are true
    and righteous altogether.

10 More to be desired are they than gold,
    yes, than much fine gold;
    sweeter also than honey and the honeycomb.
11 Moreover by them is Your servant warned,
    and by keeping them comes great reward.

Study the Word of God. Either get a study Bible or get into a Bible study. In some organized way, study the scriptures.

2   Timothy 2: 15 Study to show yourself approved by God, a workman who need not be ashamed, rightly dividing the word of truth.

God's Word can be engrafted or attached to our very souls. It can transform us.

James 1: 21 Therefore lay aside all filthiness and remaining wickedness and receive with meekness the engrafted word, which is able to save your souls.

God's ways are higher. He explains His ways to us in the Word of God so we can know them. God's Word always produces fruit. It never returns void.

Isaiah 55: 8 For My thoughts are not your thoughts,
    nor are your ways My ways,
    says the Lord.
9 For as the heavens are higher than the earth,
    so are My ways higher than your ways,
    and My thoughts than your thoughts.
10 For as the rain comes down,
    and the snow from heaven,
and do not return there
    but water the earth
and make it bring forth and bud
    that it may give seed to the sower and bread to the eater,
11 so shall My word be that goes forth from My mouth;
    it shall not return to Me void,
but it shall accomplish that which I please,
    and it shall prosper in the thing for which I sent it.

God's Word can transform us so that we can know what we should do and we can know what is pleasing to God and God's Word releases faith so that we can do it.

Romans 12: 1 I urge you therefore, brothers, by the mercies of God, that you present your bodies as a living sacrifice, holy, and acceptable to God, which is your reasonable service of worship. 2 Do not be conformed to this world, but be transformed by the renewing of your mind, that you may prove what is the good and acceptable and perfect will of God.
Get the person to invite a friend

How to pray with understanding

If you require an answer to prayer and you want to know how to get it. Read the scriptures on the topic. For instance, if you want to have a child, search scriptures promising children to God's people. If you need finances, find scriptures where God promises to prosper you.

1. Search scriptures for scriptures that have the answer to your prayer request.
2. Pray the answer by praying the scriptures over yourself.
3. Begin to thank God for supplying the answer even before it comes.
4. Rejoice as God answers your prayer and tell others how God has provided.
5. Teach others to do the same thing. God's Word can be the most effective type of prayer book because it states God's will.

Things you have learned teach to others.

2 Timothy 2: 1 So you, my son, be strong in the grace that is in Christ Jesus. 2 Share the things that you have heard from me in the presence of many witnesses with faithful men who will be able to teach others also.

PRAY AND PRAISE
ALWAYS RECEIVE PRAYER REQUESTS ALWAYS SERVE A SNACK
ALWAYS TALK AFTER YOUR LESSON, EVEN IF ONLY BRIEFLY

Journal topic – Apply the prayer of understanding or praying the scriptures in your daily devotions. Explain what you experienced. Also describe anything you have learned about the importance of words.

Sample Prayer

O Holy Spirit, set a watch over my mouth so that I only speak words on purpose and that align with your word. Holy Spirit, inspire me. Teach me. Direct me. Amen.

10 ANOINTING WITH OIL

Lesson 9
Anointing with Oil

Jesus – the living God – Holy Spirit – is the gift
I give you what I have – in the name of Jesus receive

Anointing with oil and faith is for healing. God can heal a person, spirit, soul and body.

Jesus died for our sins so that we may have salvation, eternal life. Jesus died for our healing so that we can be healed. Jesus took upon Himself all sin and sins judgements, so we could know the liberty of God and be healed and whole.

We are especially instructed to pray for the sick that they may be healed.

Jesus the Messiah fulfilled these scriptures.

Isiah 61: 1 The Spirit of the Lord God is upon me
    because the Lord has anointed me
    to preach good news to the poor;
He has sent me to heal the broken-hearted,
    to proclaim liberty to the captives,
    and the opening of the prison to those who are bound;
2 to proclaim the acceptable year of the Lord
    and the day of vengeance of our God;
to comfort all who mourn,
3   to preserve those who mourn in Zion,
to give to them beauty
    for ashes,
the oil of joy
    for mourning,
the garment of praise
    for the spirit of heaviness,
that they might be called trees of righteousness,
    the planting of the Lord,
    that He might be glorified.

Isiah 53: 4 Surely he has borne our grief
    and carried our sorrows;

Yet we esteemed him stricken,
    smitten of God, and afflicted.
5 But he was wounded for our transgressions,
    he was bruised for our iniquities;
the chastisement of our peace was upon him,
    and by his stripes we are healed.
6 All of us like sheep have gone astray;
    each of us has turned to his own way,
but the Lord has laid on him

Jesus commanded his disciples to go preach, heal and deliver people.

Matthew 10: 5 These twelve Jesus sent out, and commanded them, saying, "Do not go into the way of the Gentiles, and do not enter any city of the Samaritans. 6 But go rather to the lost sheep of the house of Israel. 7 As you go, preach, saying, 'The kingdom of heaven is at hand.' 8 Heal

The sick, cleanse the lepers, raise the dead, and cast out demons. Freely you have received, freely give.

The disciples did as Jesus commanded.
The command applies to us also.

Acts 3: 3 Now Peter and John went up together to the temple at the ninth hour, the hour of prayer. 2 A man lame from birth was being carried, whom people placed daily at the gate of the temple called Beautiful to ask alms from those who entered the temple. 3 Seeing Peter and John about to go into the temple, he asked for alms. 4 Peter, gazing at him with John, said, "Look at us." 5 So he paid attention to them, expecting to receive something from them.

6 Then Peter said, "I have no silver and gold, but I give you what I have. In the name of Jesus Christ of Nazareth, rise up and walk." 7 He took him by the right hand and raised him up. Immediately his feet and ankles were strengthened. 8 Jumping up, he stood and walked and entered the temple with them, walking and jumping and praising God. 9 All the people saw him walking and praising God. 10 They knew that it was he who sat for alms at the Beautiful Gate of the temple. And they were filled with wonder and amazement at what happened to him.

Instruction to pray for sick or those who need forgiveness or healing.

James 5: 13 Is anyone among you suffering? Let him pray. Is anyone merry? Let him sing psalms. 14 Is anyone sick among you? Let him call for the elders of the church, and let them pray over him, anointing him with oil in the name of the Lord. 15 And the prayer of faith will save the sick, and the Lord will raise him up. And if he has committed any sins, he will be forgiven. 16 Confess your faults to one another and pray for one another, that you may be healed. The effective, fervent prayer of a righteous man accomplishes much.

Prayerfully – silently or separately pray. If God reveals any area of your life where you need to forgive someone. Do it. If there is anything in you that needs healing do it. Stir up your faith so that Jesus can minister through you as you pray for the person to be healed. Pray for complete and total healing. If the Holy Spirit prompts you, obey His lead. For instance, you may know the person need to forgive someone.

Pray for healing over the person anointing him or her with oil. Place a dab of oil on the forehead and keep your hand there as you pray.

" O God, I pray healing for Name. You said to pray with faith believing and we would receive. I pray healing in the spirit, soul and body in Jesus name. Amen.

PRAY AND PRAISE
ALWAYS RECEIVE PRAYER REQUESTS ALWAYS SERVE A SNACK
ALWAYS TALK AFTER YOUR LESSON, EVEN IF ONLY BRIEFLY

Journal topic – anointing with oil – describe it's importance. Explain any revelation you received on the teaching. Explain what you can do so you have boldness to pray healing for people.

12 CONCLUSION OR TRANSITION

Lesson 10 Conclusion or transition

This could be your final meeting. It is the conclusion of this Bible study. It doesn't mean it is the conclusion to your getting together with the person. It may be. In this last get together talk over refreshments about things to come. You should review your main teachings from the study. Emphasize the importance of continuing to teach others the things we learn. Emphasize the need for personal spiritual development. Discuss options.

1. Prayer
2. Praise and worship
3. Baptism of Holy Spirit – tongues
4. Using tongues to praise and worship
5. Using tongues to pray
6. Communion
7. Foot washing – men with men, women with women
8. Serving
9. Mentoring others

At least 1 hour – no more than 2 hours.

Options

You could get the person encouraged to start discipling someone – a youth. You could encourage the person to serve in the local church or at a charity. You could get the person to start a new Bible study elsewhere. You could offer to continue with a Bible study of a Book of the Bible. Find out if the person has any other ideas for further Bible study. If the person doesn't know his or her spiritual gifts, it is an excellent next study.

You may choose an alternative to all of these.

Aim – It can be now or later but discuss your aim is that the person will teach what he or she has learned to others. Get the person to establish a small group or Bible study with at least 1 person If the person is a new Christian, you may study a book of the Bible with him or her such as the gospel of John. You may decide to offer the Bible study to the person and his or her friend. It is a way of getting him or her used to Bible study. Use various translations of the scriptures to make it easier to understand.

Deuteronomy 11: 18 Therefore you must fix these words of mine in your heart and in your soul, and bind them as a sign on your hand, so that they may be as frontlets between your eyes. 19 You shall teach them to your children, speaking of them when you sit in your house and when you walk by the way, when you lie down, and when you rise up. 20 You shall write them on the doorposts of your house and on your gates, 21 so that your days and the days of your children may be multiplied in the land which the Lord swore to your fathers to give them, as long as the days of heaven on the earth.

Encourage the person to train others. If the person has been changed by your mentoring, he or she will want to tell others the truths of God's Word.

Journal: Most important aspects of our Bible study – 3-5 things. Get the person to write it and also to discuss it with you. Inquire if the person knows his or her spiritual gifts. It would be an excellent are of study next. If your church has a class suggest it. If not, you may recommend them to a place they are taught. Rick Warren has an excellent several book Bible study on the topic of Spiritual gifts. It would similar in length to study the books in the study.

Journal topic – what you have learned through the mentoring classes and what you believe is next for you in terms of learning and serving. Explain most important things you have learned.

Make a commitment to keep a journal discussing your spiritual life. They can be scriptures or events or how God is using you.

Keep God's Word as a priority – Sow into others lives

Joshua 1: 6 "Be strong and courageous, for you shall provide the land that I swore to their fathers to give them as an inheritance for this people. 7 Be strong and very courageous, in order to act carefully in accordance with all the law that My servant Moses commanded you. Do not turn aside from it to the right or the left, so that you may succeed wherever you go. 8 This Book of the Law must not depart from your mouth. Meditate on it day and night so that you may act carefully according to all that is written in it. For then you will make your way successful, and you will be wise. 9 Have not I commanded you? Be strong and courageous. Do not be afraid or dismayed, for the Lord your God is with you wherever you go."

PRAY AND PRAISE
ALWAYS RECEIVE PRAYER REQUESTS ALWAYS SERVE A SNACK
ALWAYS TALK AFTER YOUR LESSON, EVEN IF ONLY BRIEFLY

Encourage the person to pursue God so he or she gets a RHEMA WORD from God.
Explain the importance of listening to the Holy Spirit. – Sharing from the Word.

Communion with the student.

PRAY OVER THE PERSON ON YOUR LAST FORMAL LESSON. YOU MAY MEET AFTERWARDS AS GOD LEADS YOU – IT MAY BE YOUR LAST MEETING. CONFIRM THE TRUTHS TAUGHT

Doctrines of Christ –Laying hands on the person to confirm truths learned

Hebrews 6: 1 Therefore, leaving the elementary principles of the doctrine of Christ, let us go on to maturity, not laying again a foundation of repentance from dead works and of faith toward God, 2 of instruction about washings, the laying on of hands, the resurrection of the dead, and eternal judgment. 3 This we will do if God permits.

If it is your last class with the person, pray a special blessing with him or her.

Sample Prayer

O God, Thank you for bringing Name into my life these past weeks. I pray you would confirm the things he or she has learned. Give him or her opportunities to teach others. Lead and direct him or her in ministry activities. Lead him or her in friendships and in spiritual growth. I pray blessing and favour over Name. In Jesus name. Amen.

IF YOU SERVE IN THE CHURCH, INVITE THE PERSON TO HELP YOU
ENCOURAGE THE YOUTH TO JOIN IN VOLUNTEERING IN THE CHURCH

Journal topic – personal goals for the future – spiritual, educational, career. Family

Discussion – lifelong commitment to personal spiritual growth, relationship with God, future

Conclusion

The past 9 lessons have been a study of the essential doctrines of the Charismatic Pentecostal Christian faith. The main emphasis is giving yourself wholly unto God.

Romans 12: 1 I urge you therefore, brothers, by the mercies of God, that you present your bodies as a living sacrifice, holy, and acceptable to God, which is your reasonable service of worship. 2 Do not be conformed to this world, but be transformed by the renewing of your mind, that you may prove what is the good and acceptable and perfect will of God.

By developing your relationship to mentor a student, you yourself have been used by God and have imparted into someone's life. The student's experiences and spiritual growth are evidence of your sincere investment into the Body of Christ.

You yourself have been committed to professional and spiritual development as well as mentoring someone. It is important that both you and the student realize that it is not the end of processes but a transition. It is possible for you to continue a study of a different sort. What is most essential is that the person develop faith to believe that he or she could mentor someone in the same way that he or she has been mentored. The person may become a personal friend. The person may simply be in your life for a brief period. What is necessary is that you have given your best to the person. By mentoring someone and praying for him or her continually, the person becomes important; you come to love him or her in a special way.

Giving a copy of this book or some other type of book that could be a Bible study text is highly recommended.

Assess the situation and trust God to lead you on the next steps. Also, trust the Holy Spirit to direct the person you have mentored. You should decide a future pathway of professional development and spiritual development for your own self. Consider the next steps for your own self also. Consider if you will take a new class, teach a class, research a new area.

Pray for God to lead you to the next person that you will mentor. Give all your best to those you mentor. God will reward you by the fruit they bare in their lives. You may decide that once a year you invite some of the people you have mentored to a get together. In some way connecting people in the body of Christ is enriching.

13 JOURNAL TOPICS

List of Journal Topics

List of Topics covered in the book..

Both you and the student should keep a journal of what God is doing in your life during the mentoring. You may choose to share your journals entries with each other. The topics covered in the course include the following:

1.   Prayer
2.   Praise and worship
3.   Baptism of Holy Spirit – tongues
4.   Using tongues to praise and worship
5.   Using tongues to pray
6.   Communion
7.   Foot washing – men with men, women with women
8.   Serving
9.   Mentoring others

Introduction to Journal Writing - Journal Topic Start Choose any of the following to write on. Discuss your goal for the mentorship duration.

1.   Describe for me what life is like for you at school, work, home.
2.   Music listen to
3.   Movies
4.   Tv shows
5.   Books reading or leisure activities
6.   Describe your church life, commitments,
7.   Hobbies and talents, sports, music, other
8.   Goals for yourself for the school year or semester
9.   Spiritual goals
10. Important things God has taught you
11. Instances you knew God was speaking to you or leading you
12. Instances when you knew God was using you
13. Ways you can contribute to your family, community, country
14. List spiritual gifts or any experience you directly spoke with God and you knew you were in His presence.

15.   Water baptism
16.   Baptized in the Holy Spirit

Keep a journal – of each meeting – also record any questions you want to discuss.

Give those questions to the student to write in his or her journal. You may choose some of the topics to discuss as the person feels free. He or she should only share what he or she feels comfortable sharing.

First journal : discuss any of the topics from the discussion.

Journal 1

Journal Question – write approximately 1 page. Write on these topics and any other topic the Holy Spirit has placed on your heart.

1.   Salvation
2.   Healing and/ or deliverance
3.   Being prompted by the Holy Spirit

Discuss your point of view of the get togethers. Explain anything you have learned through them or anything God is placing on your heart.

Journal 2

Journal Question

Explain any revelation you have concerning communion. Write about what God is teaching you and any aspect of your relationship with Him.

Journal 3

Journal Topic – explain how important is praise and worship to your life and if you regularly include it in your daily relationship with God. Explain your impression of today's get together on the topic of giving yourself to God wholly.

Journal 4

Discussion of importance of the Baptism of the Holy Spirit. Explain the experience and how it helps you to witness.

Journal 5

Journal Topic

Explain what you understand to be the most important aspects of covenant with Jesus. Explain what he offers and what you offer.

Journal 6

Journal Topic: describe the importance of foot washing as taught in the scriptures. Explain areas you serve or volunteer in church or areas you are interested in volunteering.

Journal 7

Journal topic – Apply the prayer of understanding or praying the scriptures in your daily devotions. Explain what you experienced. Also describe anything you have learned about the importance of words.

Journal 8

Journal topic – anointing with oil – describe it's importance. Explain any revelation you received on the teaching. Explain what you can do so you have boldness to pray healing for people.

Journal 9

Journal topic – anointing with oil – describe it's importance. Explain any revelation you received on the teaching. Explain what you can do so you have boldness to pray healing for people.

Conclusion Journal – transition to next aspect of your life.

Journal topic – personal goals for the future – spiritual, educational, career. Family

Briefly give sentences to answer the following.

Discussion – personal spiritual growth, relationship with God, future

Describe your goals for future spiritual growth. 1 year or 12 months

Describe your goals for professional development. 1 year or 12 months

Describe your goals for short term volunteering or mentoring.

Describe your goals for spiritual growth. Describe what should be next in your life.

Although this is the last journal entry, I highly encourage you to keep a journal of scriptures God is quickening to you as well as a discussion of things God is teaching you.

OTHER BOOKS BY
CHRIS A. LEGEBOW

Available on Amazon.ca Amazon.com or Kindle
Or the Create Space webstore.

By Living Word Publishers

Angels: Ministering Spirits

Discipling the Generation

An Excellent Spirit: Living Life Wholly Unto God

Covenant With God: God's Relationship With Man

Discovering and Using your Spiritual Gifts

Divine Healing in the Scriptures: God's Mercy Towards Man

Jesus Christ: Saviour, Healer, Deliverer, LORD

Kinds of Giving: From the Holy Scriptures

Signs of Jesus Coming

Spheres of Authority: Know yours

The Commandments

The Doctrine of Christ: Essential Truths of Scripture

Continued…

OTHER BOOKS BY CHRIS A. LEGEBOW

The Five-Fold Ministry: Gifts to the Church

Kinds of Prayer. Knowing Them and Using Them Effectively

Living Life Fully: Knowing your Purpose

The Anointing: the Glory of God

The High Calling: Life Worth Living

The Sacraments: A Charismatic Guide

ABOUT THE AUTHOR

Chris Legebow is a Christian Professor of English and Communications. She has taught at the elementary, high school and College and University levels. She has ministered in her local churches in intercessory prayer, teaching Sunday school and other Christian Doctrine classes to children and youth. She has preached to congregations and given her testimony. Although she was not raised in a Christian home, she came to know Jesus Christ as her Saviour and LORD while she was studying in University. This radically transformed her life in terms of priorities and commitment.

She has a strong passion for the great commission – that Jesus Christ would be preached throughout all the earth believing that it a major sign of the LORD's return. She has been a part of several different types of full gospel charismatic churches but has also gained much of her insight and enlightenment from Christian Media and broadcasting. She hopes to continue ministering, serving, interceding and giving and teaching until the LORD returns.

Manufactured by Amazon.ca
Bolton, ON

40611521R00042